Hum If You Can't Sing

GLEN BROWN

Boat House Productions
STATESVILLE, NORTH CAROLINA

Published by:
Boat House Productions

STATESVILLE, NC
boathouseproductionsnc.com
boathouseproductionsnc@gmail.com

Copyright © 2023 Glen Brown

All rights reserved. No part of this book may be reproduced or transmitted in any form or by any means, graphic, electronic, or mechanical, including photocopying, recording, taping, Web distribution, or by any informational storage and retrieval system without written permission from the author.

Library of Congress Control Number: 2023902873

ISBNs:
978-1-7372855-8-8 (hardcover)
978-1-7372855-9-5 (paperback)
978-1-7372855-1-0 (ebook)

Editing: Robert Borta, Carol Killman Rosenberg
Interior & cover design: Gary A. Rosenberg
Author photo: Gary Adam
Cover photo: Glen Brown

*For my wife, Marilyn Marie,
our children, Geoffrey Glen and Suzanne Elizabeth,
and our grandchildren*

> *"In the realm of feelings, the real and what is imaginary, assumed, pretended are hardly distinguishable"*
> —HENRI PEYRE

Contents

I

Adverbial Paradoxes 2

Bartleby the Scrivener 4

Dillinger, Alias Jimmy Lawrence 5

If Anthony Weiner Had Met Little Red Riding Hood 6

Cinderella Dancing 8

Briar Rose Defunct 9

Snow White Turns 211 11

Riding Rapunzel 12

It's More than Pheromones 13

Euclid and Barbie 15

Jeremy Bentham: "Present but Not Voting" 16

Hum If You Can't Sing 18

Because 20

II

The Billboard 22

Peter Stubbs Packs Up and Flees to Chicago via Time Machine to Escape Bad Press 23

Ripped from Space 25

The Iceman Cometh No More 27

Paolo and Francesca   28

Gifts from God   30

Sanctuary   31

Munditia, Patron Saint of Lonely Women   33

Día de los Muertos   35

Double Vision   37

The Running of the Bulls Festival   39

What Medals Also Mean   40

Cain and Cain   42

III

The Day after Vito's Tavern, Father's Day 1957   44

Elizabeth Street   46

Safe at Home   48

Just Not Fast Enough   50

Jim's Mom   52

"The Devil's Whore"   54

In the Crosshairs   55

Suburban Lockup   57

Bubbie   60

Epitaph for a Transsexual   62

A Small Plot in the Short Story of Our Lives   64

Gray Squirrels, One Robin   66

After an Argument with My Father   68

Birth of an Angel   70

IV

Keeping a Net beneath Them   74

Hell   76

"Have a Nice Day"   77

Spilt Milk   78

Obsession   80

Not Quite a Sonnet on the Divisibility of Kinetics and Infinite Bisection (or a Theory on Yard Work)   82

Considering a Cat Crossing Highway 435 at 3 a.m. in Kansas City (or Death Does Not Always Have the Right of Way)   83

The Checkup (or A Symphony for a Dental Hygienist)   84

Don't Ask Why   86

COVID-19 at the Grocery Store   88

Grocery Lists   89

"Plaudite, Amici, Comoedia Finita Est"   90

Without Pomp and Circumstance   92

Acknowledgments   97

About the Author   101

I

Adverbial Paradoxes

Yes

It's the high five of words
with a swish of sound,
an affirmation of what is
and what might come.
In one small breath,
it can change us with its pledge.
Its covenant, sometimes superstitious,
like crossing one's heart
or kissing the Book,
locks us to the future.

Yes is the adverbial wishbone of fate,
an affidavit of hope,
washing, like a tidal wave,
politics into history,
geography into space.

No

We say it when all else fails,
and we are at nerve's end.
It's a proud word with an emphatic O
and said with light speed.
The exclamation bursts
like a dark fist from our tongues.

No is an unambiguous disclaimer,
shouting miles away from *maybe*,

light years from *yes*.
It's a stubborn word
bellowing from the larynx and oral cavity.
Yet, *no* needs repeating
like learning a foreign language
or the multiplication table for the first time.

It's a saucy adverb,
the least breath of sound,
smarting like jalapeños against the palate,
and it leaves no doubt.

Maybe

It's a word full of promise, a word like sex
ringing with possibility
like a second, sidelong glance,
a cousin of *perhaps*, a distant relative of *chance*
with no present, without guarantee,
a nondescript meaning with a built-in mortality
but more alluring than *yes*
and not as confident as *no*.

Maybe puts us on parole, sentencing us
with ellipses, hurling us into doubt
where imagination becomes as thrilling
as the goal itself. It's a word ready to lie,
an adverbial paradox full of hope.
It keeps us hungry, and we say it
to our children and loved ones
because it's less harsh than *no*
but not quite *yes*, knowing all along
it will be one or the other.

Bartleby the Scrivener

"Ah, Bartleby! Ah, Humanity!"
—HERMAN MELVILLE

Perhaps he lost the language of desire,
hope checking out first
with its twin baggage of *want* and *need*,
hunger leaving no forwarding address.

Or maybe the language of etiquette
surrendered its meaning,
the tongue holding *diplomacy* hostage
behind a green folding screen.

Let's presume he was stunned into silence
by God's loneliness, by the fixed glare
of the black wall just beyond
the small side window courting a dim light.

So much to "prefer not to" while the grass
and sky stitched together a singular void,
and the bud of existentialism took root
deep within his heart, *denial* sprouting

against the dead letters and bricks
that merged into a mortuary of self-interest.
He knew nothingness soon becomes a stranger
to no one, preferring it was his last resistance.

Dillinger, Alias Jimmy Lawrence

He walked out into a night
delirious with moonshine,
the woman's perfume suddenly lifting
from his arms—all sure signs of death.
What seemed like a good idea
rewound his brief life's history.

This time he had no wooden gun for escape,
no forceps to flip his tongue,
to bring him back from the dead
like a gangster Lazarus.
Only Anna Sage knew who he was. He told her
his Depression-day Robin Hood stories,
but she preferred Indiana to Romania.

Not until the moment he left the Biograph Theater
right after Melvin Purvis lit a cigar,
called out his real name,
did a kind of alley loneliness
rise like a red skirt of darkness
then exit his right eye for good.

If Anthony Weiner Had Met
Little Red Riding Hood

(Anthony Weiner is a former member of Congress who had been involved in multiple sex scandals related to sexting.)

The plot is flawed; the dialogue is unbelievable.
The wolf lacks a compulsive trait.
Why not make him a politician
with an addictive sexting problem
and pump him up with arrogance and a stump speech?
As for Red, wearing a velvet coat,
black tights, satin blouse, and high heels,
just add a pouting mouth, legs of a runway model
and the endurance of a triathlon athlete.

Now put them somewhere downtown in Manhattan
with the Budweiser horses panting
around a clock in a smoke-filled bar,
blaring music and six-dollar beer calls.
And let's say she doesn't have a florist's heart
for long-stemmed roses or daffodils,
or drink imported wines or eat French pastries.
Instead, she's smitten by the scent of loud cologne,
dizzy with come-ons and roving hands—
their conversation stale as the popcorn and Frito-Lays.
We know the odds, perhaps ten thousand to one,
like the first day of major league baseball tryouts.
But he's determined and she's willing,
lust floating in his brain and love in hers.

Oh, I'll spare you the happiness forever after
and little-lost-girl-saved-by-a-prince routine.
There is no rise in concentration
of some polypeptide hormone
in his hypothalamus. Besides, he's married.
They wake up with separation swirling in their hearts,
lost in a forest of ordinary in the haze of day,
lying with the promise to see each other
before his next mayoral debate.
He rises out of bed, taps a text message
on his iPhone, counts the bills in his billfold
to make sure, then straightens his tie
while she brushes her hair, her bare arm
twitching as the door clicks shut.

Cinderella Dancing

In America, it's black high-tops,
and cobbler's wax won't hold them down.
She drives a red Ford Focus in a vinyl mini,
works night shifts at Corrugated Box Incorporated
for twice minimum wage.
On weekends, she twerks with her prince
'til dawn, her brow boiling like ethanol,
her feet tireless on the dance-hall parquet.
She burns her lust to cinders,
sleeps among the ashes to noon
in a brass-framed bed.

This is a new-world doll locked in uppercase,
rolling boyfriends like stones.
There are no hazel twigs for her devotions,
no pigeon houses or pear trees to hide in,
just Houdini wrapped in a straitjacket of Self,
born into a world already made to order.

Briar Rose Defunct

There's not much he can say to a woman,
who believes she's slept for 100 years,
launched from a century of dreams with just a kiss.
It doesn't matter, and besides her breath is bad.

Outside, condos have erupted from the ground,
and the evening sky is freckled with fewer stars.
Inside, he hands her a long-stemmed rose.
It's thornless, and he asks her to marry him,
knowing that no insurance company
will cover another coma like this one.

With "Who the hell are you?" bursting from her lips,
brittle with the senselessness of ice,
he knows the anesthetic has worn off,
but her amnesia hasn't.

It makes him think about the physics in all of this,
the coming light about to pour
through a hole in her universe,
how evolution will never be the same.

Even so, he cannot remember
how the story is supposed to end:
why the flies were asleep on the walls
and the horses in their stables,
the brindled hounds in the yard, even the doves,
their heads tucked under their wings.

Although that was another tale,
it doesn't take long for him to discover
that nothing consoles quite like an eternity
of dreamless nights as she drones
something about insomnia . . .

He slips out of the room, his knees spilling
into a gurney veering down the hall
with the white sheet pulled over,
his hands grasping the answer in an instant.

Snow White Turns 211

Oh, Snow White, eternal housewife,
you should have danced all night
in your stepmother's red-hot iron shoes.
She knew that a woman's face mattered enough
to tell lies, worked her own with Oil of OLAY.
Did you think the men in your life
would not want a beautiful housewife too?

You should have married that huntsman instead
and slept on the forest floor, or lived
with the wild boar, and saved your heart
from boundless hours of housework
and whoring for those seven little men,
and the moments in between while you watched
your sigh-long tale of woe thickened like cold porridge.

Had you puked out the last of your luck
when your prince arrived,
the teakettle would not be steaming
with anger and misting old desires
while your hands conspired
against the polygraphic lines around your eyes
reflected in the looking glass upon your wall.

Riding Rapunzel

One day a beautiful woman bolted out
of bewildering love,
exited the wider circumference
of her loneliness,
and threw down her golden hair
over her dove-white breasts
for men to climb for trysts.

She galloped into their lives
like the trumpet's shocking blare
at the starting gate,
built a small fire in each of their hearts
until one day she broke her stride,
cantered upon the thin ice
of an early thaw of marriage,
and drowned herself in a blue tower—
the mistress of sad fairy-tale luck.

It's More than Pheromones

*"I admit without shame
I'm talking about superficial beauty."*
—STEPHEN DUNN

They are not
like other women,
and they know it.
They make us tremble,
hold our breath, wheel
and fantasize.
Everything is put on hold
when they enter a room.
Motion defies time,
and we moan.

They suffer
for this special advantage,
for needing our reassurance,
and we know
that it's better to treat them
as if they were
unexceptional,
like the middling girl next door.
They'll be surprised
by our indifference, relieved
of having to put forth
another effort.

They might allow us to approach,
attend to what we might ask of them,
offer us their loneliness
in return for not imploring.
And lucky we will be
to have had such women
in our lives,
when years from now
we unplug our lust
and drift perpetually in memory.

Euclid and Barbie

"Math class is tough."
—BARBIE

Sure, it doesn't add up:
countless camping and skiing trips with Ken,
swimming and skating parties without danger,
dancing and shopping engagements
with Midge and Skipper
like an infinite summer vacation.
Nothing here hints at a dull math class
for integral Barbie and her complex playmates!
Even her curvaceous body
proves mathematically impossible.
She's an isosceles bimbo
with the whole greater than the sum of her parts.
Just bend her at an obtuse angle,
press her into her pink Porsche
and watch her scud across miles of linoleum
or catapult down the stairs.
You'll know that her appeal
is an equation of Euclidean beauty and speed.
She doesn't need school.
She was created to multiply
fantasy by freedom in every young girl's mind.
Why be upset when Barbie says,
"Math class is tough"?
You can always add for her—
the numberless accessories
to her version of the American dream.

Jeremy Bentham: "Present but Not Voting"

(He left his entire estate to the University College in London with the provision that his remains be preserved and present at all meetings of the board.)

He was hooked on Latin at three years old,
became a reader of Han Fei, Helvétius,
Hutcheson, Hartley, and Hume.
"I felt as if scales had fallen from my eyes,"
he said of Hume's *A Treatise of Human Nature*.

He was an English sympathizer
of the American Revolution;
utilitarian, codifier, social reformer,
and patron saint of animal rights,
but clumsy lover with women—
it might have been Asperger's
during those fog of days at the university.

He was robotic as the rain
on the windows of his study,
obsessed with his "greatest happiness" principle
and "calculus of felicity."

It was said he left manuscripts
of more than 30 million words,
but only one short request
before passing through the clogged lungs
of an early nineteenth century:

that his head be placed under an air pump
of flowing sulfuric acid—
in the craze of South American headhunters—
to capture his soul;
that his skeleton be padded with hay,
dressed in his clothes, and positioned upon a chair
so his mummified self could attend meetings
of the College Council
and be listed through posterity
as "present but not voting."

Hum If You Can't Sing

So, what if at every conflict in life we burst
into song—thoughtless as reciting a prayer—

reward our feet with a waltz or two,
congratulate ourselves with an aria

then tap dance our way through
the kitchen and dining room?

And suppose the musicians arrive early
each morning to tune up their strings

and oil their drums
while the white-gloved conductor waits

with his cue sheet at the breakfast table?
Would we expect a chorus prophesying disaster

or a fugue in D-minor?
Why not ask for a drum roll through toiletry instead

or a diminuendo through dinner?
And what might our friends and spouse say

about all that sheet music stuffed in our pockets,
about our lives cluttered with voice lessons,

rehearsals and women dressed in high heels
and fishnet stockings?

Imagine the fun of it all, the spotlight
on us all as we dance and sing

throughout our lives with our pets joining in
with happy tails, and birds whistling

from their cages, encouraging applause
for our pitch-perfect responses each day.

Because

It's an echo of the question why,
a boomerang of logic, the reason
for punching the little girl's arm,
for breaking her new doll.

And bullies say it
with firecracker snap, owl-eyed
and with the whack and thump
of an eighteenth-century beheading.

Because is all the reason they need,
the way out of the pickle, the password
for the storybook door, the answer
to why the chicken crossed the road.

II

The Billboard

(after Philip Larkin)

"Come Dine at the Luxurious Hotel Langham"
lured an eye-choking woman
who lay pasted across the billboard.
She was unyielding in her bossy green

two-piece ensemble with strategic studs.
A bottle of wine stood between
her legs and dirigibles
that hovered over the linguini.

She was glued one day in April.
Within a week, her huge
papered crotch and thighs
held hen tracks of hieroglyphic genitalia.

It didn't take long for the great modest tear
that left only a sliver of flesh
under a colossal glass of wine
and monstrous loaf of bread,

crumbs the size of golf balls over which now read:
"Jesus of Nazareth Requests
the Honor of Your Presence
at a Dinner to be Given in His Honor."

Peter Stubbs Packs Up and Flees to Chicago via Time Machine to Escape Bad Press

Imagine somewhere in Chicago
Stubbs takes out the folded newspaper ad
stuffed loosely in his shrunken trousers
with growling, snarling defiance,
his restless, furtive eyes glowing
under the hazy light of the full moon.
"Call a Gregory Clinic today for permanent removal
of unwanted facial and body hair . . ." it reads.

What could this be? he wonders.
He had petitioned Beelzebub before.
He'd even omitted parsley from his cauldron
of opium, hemlock, and henbane,
hoping for smoother, hair-free skin.
Now he was just a phone call away.

Imagine his brilliant, white teeth flashing
beneath his yellow-green eyes,
dark patches of fur standing on end
as he reads about the International Academy
of Professional Electrologists, modern alchemists
and their new state-of-the-art technology.

More effective than rye, mistletoe, and yew,
he muses for a moment. It's time to escape
the threat of decapitation that lycanthropy and folklore
had contrived for more than four hundred years . . .

Stubbs paces wildly in circles.
He rolls around in the dirt three times,
then dusts off his soiled trousers.
The clouds traverse suddenly, illuminating
a Hunter's moon, just as he begins to dial . . .

Ripped from Space

*"Sergei Krikalev, a cosmonaut, remained in space
because there was not enough money
to bring him back to earth.
After a 10-month marathon,
the fellow who couldn't even score
some honey was finally home."*
—*from a news story*

When Sergei Krikalev returned
to the barren steppes of Kazakhstan,
reeking of horseradish and lemons,
he knew he had traveled the length
of more than one revolution,
that he had come back a galactic victim
of economic relativity to a world
now bewitched by a game of Wolfenstein
instead of a game of ninepin,
while he had orbited 200 miles above the earth.

When he heard the yoke of communism had broken
and that his space station nearly sold
to the highest bidder,
his knees locked together; his eyes rolled back.

So they set him down in a wooden chair
to take his pulse and wipe his brow.
And after they weatherproofed him
with fur to riffle back the wind
that gray day in spring,

he rubbed his eyes like Rip Van Winkle,
not knowing another revolution had taken place
where he now found himself
whilst the lone loyal subject
lost in liberty, moonstruck
with the thought that he could finally score
honey in some place unlike heaven.

The Iceman Cometh No More

*"He was snatched from death completely outfitted
with the implements of everyday existence 5,300 years ago
on the border between Austria and Italy . . .
except for penis and scrotum."*
—from a news story

Had the sloe berry and mushroom eater
arisen from his carved stillness
amid an ejaculation of protests

over custody rights in a room too bright to focus,
he may have groped for his lucky charm
to uncast the spell, known what to barter:

copper ax and rucksack for tissue and pouch.
But curiosity erected a jackhammer's sadness,
and refrigerator's hum, found a table souvenir

like a displaced part of desire
at the edge of a melting glacier,
the leather quiver without an arrow.

Paolo and Francesca

*"A history teacher took a novel approach
to dealing with a student who fell asleep in class:
he licked the student's ear."*

—*from a news story*

"That day we read no further."
—CANTO V, CIRCLE 2: THE INFERNO

Don't fall asleep in Mr. Henry's class.
He'll lick your ear clean
with unblinking eyes and feline agility.

He teaches history for pay,
tongues earwax for free.
He brings mystic lore from home,
Egyptian magic and talismans,
voluptuous lapping and a mysterious
sense of propriety.

Perhaps it was the waning moon
eaten away by field mice
that prompted Mr. Henry to arch his back
and purr while he licked that ear.

But someone did not like
Mr. Henry's skulking as the mythic
cat of the classroom.

The school board found him indiscreet;
the students found it peculiar
that their classmate remained
in a passionate embrace with Morpheus
on the dark forests of a history text.

A small pool of spit
drowned the other lesson of the day.

Gifts from God

*"Joseph Reinholtz, after making a pilgrimage
to Medjugorje, was divinely directed
to Queen of Heaven Cemetery, where he was healed
from blindness before a cross that some say bleeds,
changes color, and turns rosaries to gold."*

—from a news story

They are discovered on tortillas
or in bowls of breakfast cereals,
on cankered walls in distant villages,
or in bowling alleys and on strands of pasta
printed on Pizza Hut billboards—
these messages of fasting, faith, and peace,
gifts from God to the devotees
of the Roman Catholic Archdiocese.
But this is the place of miracles now:
Hillside, Illinois, at the Queen of Heaven
Cemetery, where people drop by
before tennis and brunch at the Oakbrook Mall
to watch their rosaries turn to 14k gold
with just a Midas prayer
before a bleeding, chameleonic cross
far from the villages
where sins are forgiven just for devotion,
and a diet of cures and conversions
is served for the faithful each day
before a weeping Virgin icon.

Ask Joseph Reinholtz.
He saw it with his own eyes.

Sanctuary

*"A naked man, carrying red carnations,
ran into St. Patrick's Cathedral . . .
He killed one man and injured a police officer
before being shot to death."*

—*from a news story*

We might imagine him
straight edging his wrists
or plunging from bridge to water,
a .22 ricocheting off the back of his skull
or his feet dangling above the oak wood floor.

Instead, he chose absolution
by way of another form of suicide.
He took off his clothes
at 51st Street and 5th Avenue
and entered the Manhattan shrine
where the air was charged with incense,
the votive candles flickered yellowish orange,
and the inscrutable, soft murmurings
of prayer rose above the front pews.

The parishioners gasped
when the brass stanchion
crushed down upon the usher's back,
as he believed he was Christ
purging his temple from sinners
while chanting dark monologues
to exorcise demons.

He discarded his life on the streets
because he wanted to find something
more impossible: testimony, refuge, God.

He was gunned down in the middle aisle
of St. Patrick's Cathedral among the flowers
and the faithful, his sepulcher
spilling blood at the foot of the altar.

Munditia, Patron Saint of Lonely Women

(Saint Munditia is believed to have been martyred in 310 A.D., beheaded with a hatchet. Once kept hidden in a wooden box, her relics were put on display in 1883. Each year, on November 17th, a feast day is held in her honor complete with a High Mass and candle procession at St. Peter's Church in Munich.)

for M.K.

She was propped up one day
in a black-and-silver sepulcher
with an eternal glass view,
her vest sewn with gaudy charms,
her gloved hands clutching a chalice
half-filled with sand
and a long golden feather.

How difficult to look at those eyes,
fixed in a perpetual stare mocking death,
at her stone-studded skeleton
encased in glass, and to think
about her estranged life,
a lifetime devoted to Christ, her ex-lover,
and how you said:
"Poor, pitiful woman cheated by faith
and her celibate single-mindedness."

And then to imagine that someone
could bejewel her, knowing all along
that her most precious gem,
her locus of power,
had rotted away to bone
where "even from the tomb
the voice of nature cries."

Día de los Muertos

*"At least 41 worshippers were suffocated
or crushed to death in Chalma, Mexico,
when a tightly packed crowd began pushing
and shoving at a church famed for a religious icon
believed to have miraculous powers.
Thirteen of the victims were children."*
—from a news story

They came from Guadalupe and Guasave
and from villages in the south
with prayer on their tongues,
across nameless plains and mountains
in borrowed automobiles full of parcels
of hope and faith, their lives pawned
for one more pilgrimage.

Little children in their Sunday suits
and starched white cotton dresses;
young, barefooted women
in embroidered bodices and lacy headdresses;
their mustachioed men in huaraches and doeskin;
and the old: tortilla-breasted and stern-faced
in dark shawls, fingering beads, pressed together.

Like a pile of sapodilla seeds,
they gathered at the sanctuary
with garlands of marigolds and chrysanthemum,
hoping for a cure.

There was a loud perfume of bougainvillea
rising among the festoons,
the Virgin enticing them to come closer,
and then an avalanche of bodies—
the terrible stomping
and crushing of skulls and bones—
two and a half tons of piety
beneath the shrine, one afternoon
under the hemorrhaging Mexican sun,
the red sky burning in their eyes.

Double Vision

"Venezuelan police arrested a doctor and eleven
city morgue employees in Caracas on suspicion of removing
the eyes from corpses and selling them for corneal transplants
to a doctor in Maracay who was charging up to $2,000."
    —*from a news story*

Now that he has new eyes,
a mosaic of phosphenes
becomes his corneal slideshow.
The scarlet ibis, cuckoo, and Orinoco crocodile,
some ten million different color surfaces
emerge in an Andes panorama.

But suppose he's a rich white man
in Maracay with these dry mestizo eyes,
these freedom-fighter eyes
with a retina of debt and anger.
Will they flash high-rise ranchos
or sharecropping black gold
from Lake Maracaibo?
Does he dine with the provincial elite,
protesting the socialist with a master plan?

And suppose while staring
into his vegetable stew, plantains,
cacao, and slabs of beef
or while dancing the joropo
his optic nerves trigger the insides
of a squatter settlement outside Caracas

or the faces of children in barrios
across coastal lowlands.

Maybe he sees an ophthalmologist
for artificial tears
or a psychiatrist for photophobia.
Maybe he kneels before
a Roman Catholic priest
or the weeping Madonna
begging for the miracle
of eyes that cry.

The Running of the Bulls Festival

> *"Two bulls broke from the pack and gored
> a man and a woman on the second day
> of the annual Running of the Bulls festival
> in Pamplona, Spain."*
>
> —*from a news story*

There must have been a moment
just before the bulls began their turbocharging,
and right after Urban Troll and Anne Ruan
were tossed in the air—their bodies
bursting like piñatas—when they thought
about the hugeness of their mistake,

about the bulls' blind desire to run
and maim anything that got in their way—
their horns hooking into flesh and bone,
leaving eight-inch gashes for exits,
while the spectators gasped in horror
among the red bandanas and papier-mâché.

It must have been a time when they felt like deer
running ahead of Weimaraners,
when the four-leaf clover also lost its luck,
and the rabbit gave up its other foot.

What Medals Also Mean

*"No one looks at you as you pass
because you're a dead man until you return."*
—UNKNOWN

for L.J.

You're on the next search-and-destroy patrol
somewhere near a river.
You feel only the heat and your weariness,
the humidity and your thirst.

You can't see through the squall,
but you keep walking through the gray sheets,
beneath a canopy of contorted vegetation,
along some twisted, dirt road.

You're aware of the sucking mud
under your boots,
the elephant grass and the leeches.

And you're thinking ambush and mines,
about removing the tape
from the spoon of your grenade.

No one talks about the cobras and vipers,
the mosquitoes like an artillery burst,
the rioting stillness that follows.

You've seen a thousand nameless places,
and each time it's no different:
you fear getting lost,
that your weapon won't work.

But it's the quota that propels you on,
and you drag the bodies out in a row
to be searched, then photographed.

And you'd rather be on the perimeter
than riding an assault wave through this camp,
smelling of smoke, gunpowder, and death—
Heli-lifted for a Purple Heart.

Cain and Cain

> *"We are sitting in the silence, still.*
> *Silence, like the bullet that's missed us, spins."*
> —ILYA KAMINSKY

We, too, sit in silence,
horror-struck by raucous skies
suffused with bursts of terror,
where billows rise behind upturned thumbs
while the world tilts from an invasion
choking with fiery air and scorched earth.

And we are shown the artillery
and the brutality in daily doses:
the blasted buildings, family photographs
and children's toys blackened by fire;
mothers and their children
going to nowhere
and dead bodies everywhere.

And we go on with our lives, still,
far away from spinning ballistic arcs
of light, shattered glass and concrete,
foreboding clouds of hydrogen sulfide,
cluster and vacuum bombs.

And we send our prayers and emoticons,
well wishes and money, while America
delivers death-dealing weaponry
and continues to bomb countries of color
not worthy of world news.

III

The Day after Vito's Tavern, Father's Day 1957

for my sister "Pidge"

He was a left-handed Tarzan
swinging from Andante's grocery store awning.
His right hand waved a .22 caliber pistol,
and shots rang out on Elizabeth and Race Streets,
Father's Day 1957.

The Everly Brothers were singing
"Bye, Bye Love" on the Philco;
Rocky Marciano abandoned his title
the year before,
and this was just another Sunday brawl
between Mom and Dad.

The day after Vito's Tavern brought no surprises
for my sister and me, but this time
Mom broke my plastic guitar over his head,
heavy with 80-proof,
and we had to duck through alleys
and down gangways
to avoid his Ford Fairlane's squealing tires.

Why was he chasing us?
How was I to know about the effects
of Early Times Kentucky whiskey
and Blatz beer at six years old?

He tried to leave Mom before,
and he made my sister lug suitcases
down the stairs while I listened to cursing
and the neighbors' listening,
their doors slightly ajar.

We cried because of his almost leave-taking,
but he passed out just in time,
and my sister dragged his suitcases
up the stairs until next time.

Mom didn't speak to him for four days,
and he made me his mediator
with a mission to obtain her mercy.
By Saturday, the two of them were going to Vito's,
and "All Shook Up" was playing
on Dick Clark's *American Bandstand*.

Elizabeth Street

I went back to a place
where we used sewer covers for bases,
broomsticks for bats, and crushed wax cups
for baseballs—a place peopled with names
like Aiellinello, Petrelli and Pascucciello.

But now there are condominiums
where a cold-water walk-up once flanked
a textile factory just beyond an alleyway.

For ten summers, a street-corner fire hydrant
surged high fliers made with tires and two-by-fours.
I played along street curbs
filled from backed-up sewers until the cops
came with their monkey wrenches.

Where have the Italian feasts gone,
the marching oompah band
on Sunday mornings,
and Santa Maria Addolorata's procession
of religious icons that I was lifted up
to kiss for just one dollar?

And where is Andante's grocery store
where we pitched pennies under an awning
until dusk to escape the widening June sun
already burning away thoughts of school,
while an old man yelled, "Bunch of potatoes!"

on a horse-driven wagon
filled with fruits and vegetables
rounding Rosa's candy store,
where we bought black licorice sticks,
Kayo, and Yo-Ho potato chips
for just fifteen cents?
"I weep like a child for the past."

Safe at Home

We're playing under a blinking streetlamp
and a few luminous city stars.
First base is a sewer cover
where Race Street line-drives into Elizabeth.
Second base is Michael Petrelli's dago tee.
Third base is my dad's plumbing rag,
and home plate is my mom's dish towel.
The ball is a crushed waxed paper cup
filled with pieces of rubber,
and the bat is the handle
of a whisk brush broom.
Pitcher's hands are out.
There are no foul lines, except
for street curbs, and anything that hits
Andante's grocery store awning is a homer.
In my mind, I'm playing in Comiskey Park
at 35th & Shields against the Yankees.
My cleats are high-top Converse sneakers
with Little Louie's number 11
Sharpied on the white rubber toe caps.
The game is tied,
and my mom is broadcasting
"Get your ass home" signals
through the window blinds.

But I'm in a pickle: there are two outs,
and Jo-Jo Lucenti is on third.
I know I'll never launch one, even though
I point just like the Babe in 1932,
and I flash the hit-and-run sign instead
and lay down a bunt
that drops like a chipped marble.
And I run faster
than the "Commerce Comet,"
then all the way home, faster
than herky-jerky Duncan can run
after bearing down on me with his sinker,
and faster than my mom's countdown from ten,
where at the top of the hallway stairs
of our cold-water flat, she asks me
where her dish towel is.
I tell her it's safe at home.

Just Not Fast Enough

I tied a league ball in it,
roped it around twice with jute twine
after greasing the pocket with Vaseline,
and stuffed it in between
my mattress and box spring each fall.
By spring, my Wilson A2020
"Nellie" Fox baseball glove
was primed for another season.

Through May and June,
the days rang with "Hey, batter, batter.
Swing batter, swing!"
I swung a Duke Snider Adirondack,
but I was Luis Aparicio at the plate—
a singles hitter and fast—
a sure steal on the base paths.

In one game, the rain fouled up
my fifth stealing attempt
when second base became a buoy.
The game was called,
and my father and I
navigated out of the bog
in his new 1964 Oldsmobile Starfire,
until he asked about my muddy spikes.

We torpedoed across traffic
and slid across shoals.
He popped open the trunk
and hurled them high into the air.
I watched the long, mucky laces
of my shoes twist in slow-motion
until they hit Dempster Street
with a dull splash.

I held my breath for an eternity;
as if dreaming, I dodged
the gloom of headlights
with one last resolve
to swipe one last time,
until the entire season
suddenly disappeared five times
beneath a tractor trailer's tires.

Jim's Mom

I rode my bike to Jim's house
to play All★Star Baseball
on hot summer mornings,
rang his doorbell twice
and waited for him to answer.

But this time,
the window sheers parted slightly
and Jim's mom opened the door
wearing only a silken half-slip
and brassiere.

The shell of the wall phone
pressed against her ear
and long blond hair,
wet from bathing.
She said Jim wasn't home,

and I was embarrassed
by her large
green eyes
that flashed no hint
of awkwardness,

by her body,
like one of those models
in the lady's lingerie section
of a mail-order catalogue,
that stirred untimely yearnings.

Perhaps it was my stuttering
or her understanding
of a young boy's gawking
that made her smile sweetly
then laugh.

Even so, my body flushed
down to my toes.
And I ran home
burnt by the moment,
my bike tire still spinning
by her door.

"The Devil's Whore"

Nothing could have prepared us
for that first day of class:
our libidos impaled suddenly
by a film of copulating mantises
behind a Chinese elm,
the female's slender body
with wings like leaves,
rotating head and bulging eyes.

We soon discovered the thorax of love,
how her posture of praying
and quivering foreplay
turned to a quick thrust of spiny forelegs,
locking him in a cloak of bug lust.

We could not help but wonder
what drew him to her
for his one flight of ecstasy,
how he could continue to copulate
long after his head was devoured
by her biting mandibles.
"The Devil's Whore," the teacher called her.

No one asked the question,
and we filed quietly out of the room.
The girls, whispering,
appeared to sway down the hall
while we quickly passed them, bug-eyed.

In the Crosshairs

For five days the buck hung
from the wrought-iron grate,

a large, brown buck, heavy with muscle.
Its eyes held the look of an animal

about to be shot.
Raymond Benedetti, a pharmacist,

with a half-dozen hunting dogs
smelling of musk-rank fur,

worked his knife into its belly,
unknotting entrails before my eyes.

It wasn't until the fifth day
that someone complained

about the stench and sound
of the chainsaw grinding through bone,

about the head that lay
on the front stoop one evening,

its deciduous antlers hacked from the skull.
I watched as a young boy would, an accomplice,

under a pale gray, Midwestern sky
deep in November.

The neighbor's cats kept their distance.
The air was charged with pity and thanksgiving.

Suburban Lockup

The door handle was at eye level;
the deadbolts: where the doorknob
should have been.
The wrought-iron storm door
held in fears.
Everything was keyed from inside,
including the metal grates
across the basement windows.

They propped up a mannequin
on their vinyl couch
before they left the house—
a dummy in a black wig and kimono,
the *National Enquirer* folded on its lap.

The neighborhood voyeur
might have been aroused
had he peeked through the glass.
The night burglar might have thought
the occupants were kinky, or just lunatics
with a shotgun's trigger
wired to spring from a moving hinge.

The German Shepherd growled
from its cage at every least sound.
She could grind bones down with animal ease.

Legs would have been no contest for her,
just pretzel sticks in a salivating vise grip,
had she escaped her paddock.

There was nothing here worth stealing:
the living room sparkled silver and gold
like a sixties Slingerland drum set:
a medley of Montgomery Ward's furnishings—
plastic-covered couch and chairs,
a marble table, hurricane lamps,
and a statue of Moses
with his Ten Commandments
were among bric-a-bracs
scattered in strata.

A five-foot statue of *Rebecca at the Well*
stood at the main entrance.
The door was bolstered by a wooden cane
that buttressed the door handle,
just beneath two deadbolts
and sliding chain lock.
The dining room reflected
flock wallpaper and brown wainscot
from the smoky mirrors.

The house was eclipsed by awnings
and a fortress of evergreens,
an invitation for the random thief
from the street
to test its labyrinth of alarms,
its ambush of latches
constructed from fears
triggered by the Great Depression,
the Great War, and the nightly news—
a million hands warming over garbage cans,
hungry eyes in ski masks.

Bubbie

I imagine her escaping Ukraine,
like a small bird
breaking formation over unfamiliar terrain,
carrying her belongings in a wooden wagon
under a roof of vagrant stars
and sleeping beneath a shawl of leaves.

She bartered away her possessions in Proskuriv,
salvaged them from her hotel sacked by Cossacks
during the Bolshevik Revolution.
She gave up an old world to find a new one
more than five thousand miles away.
It was the prelude of a new life,
and the world lay before her like a matryoshka.

In America, she gave up her surname.
And though she spoke no English,
she learned the language of a new place
while keeping the old one alive.

I feel only sadness now, for her
coming so far to everything
but having nothing,
bringing with her the voice
of an old country with quiet suffering.

The Great War had murdered her family
and her husband's family
with gas and guns, and for years
she remained silent as a sleepwalker.
Her husband died too before I was born.
She seldom mentioned his name,
and I did not know how to ask.

I still remember her voice,
the way my young son used to search
in soft broken tones for the right word,
mispronouncing a vowel or consonant.
A long time ago, she would have
called my son "Doll Face."
He is the only one to carry forth our name.

Epitaph for a Transsexual

for John-David

He liked feminine things
as far back as I can remember:
high-heeled shoes, scarves, purses,

dancing before mirrors.
School was a horror.
He preferred hopscotch to relay races,

jump rope to baseball.
I imagine a woman in search of her body,
a hijacked plane touched down

in a strange place,
or a photograph of someone else
in unfamiliar clothes.

He played out his life in a foreign film
with no subtitles, with no critics
to rave in reviews, no one

to laud his impersonation.
He was less reality than dream,
more imagination than possibility,

and he lived a life without a plot
and point of view,
like a poorly written story

filled with questions and no answers.
I think of a woman I did not know,
of a sister I wish I had.

A Small Plot in the Short Story of Our Lives

We went to her home to celebrate
her sixty-fourth.
My father made dinner,
and when my sister arrived
we sang "Happy Birthday."

We looked for signs,
without knowing what to look for.
We ate her favorite cake, pineapple cheese,
disguised with whipped cream.
She opened gifts,
and my sister's youngest son
brought a bright burst
of red-and-white carnations
in a small blue vase,
delicate as our hope.

I read a few poems
about Elizabeth and Race Streets,
a small plot in the short story of our lives,
and we believed that we once lived recklessly
but in a more sensible time,
that sorrow will belong to all of us
at the end of our lives.

She was wearing her new wig,
and I thought about her
lying on the gurney, the long tube in her nose
that filled her lungs with water,
and how they rinsed her kidneys for four hours
before they dripped cisplatin and vinblastine
through a needle in her vein,
slowly as an hourglass.

She did not want to tell us
about her headaches and nausea,
that her arms bruised easily as peaches,
and how her fingertips tingled.
But we asked her,
and we trespassed on her life,
not knowing that her denouement
lay just beyond her next birthday.

Gray Squirrels, One Robin

My mother, her head sinking into pillows,
curses squirrels—
their high-wire act,
these other lives hanging
in the balance,
crossing telephone cable
hooked to the house
above the bedroom window.

For days they made her flash
accents of life.
"They keep me awake all day long,
running on the roof," she'd say.

My father, his old legs wobbling on rungs,
traps squirrels
off the pitched roof—
the cage held tightly in one hand,
the trip wire set,
smeared with peanut butter.
"I caught eleven and one robin,"
he said. "I brought them
to the cemetery and let them go."

Now she enters her long residence
at Maryhill. The robin remains,
its bold breast blazing through the bony tree.
My father and I listen for gray squirrels.
"They'll never come back," I say.

After an Argument with My Father

for Geoffrey Glen

I tell my son there are things
one should never say, hurtful words,
like *liar* and *cheat*.

*The heart holds whatever it hears
for a long time,* I say.
The tongue is the mind's fist.

I want to find the right words
to make a difference
for the wrong ones,

if recovering from them is possible,
to tell him some things from my heart
I have never said to anyone.

I can tell him what it felt like
to carry his grandmother
down the stairs after she died,

how once while sitting by her bedside
I was punched into silence
as I watched her sip

from an imaginary teacup,
how each day is an act of forgiveness,
and that the mind will know

only what it has learned
but is last to discover
what the heart has known forever.

But I know this talk is for me.
Metaphor bleeds through the words
while he stares out the passenger's window.

Birth of an Angel

for Suzanne Elizabeth

The first big snow of the year
bursts with laughter in the backyard,

the forsythia and dogwood capsizing
under the weight where his daughter

plays in a white maze of discovery,
her small arms sweeping wings

under a moon-swept sky.
He feels creation in his heart,

the mill-wheel spin,
the birth of a child without sin.

Millions of hexagons drift from heaven,
a mysterious map of the universe

hidden in each eye
spiraling toward infinity,

while the weak January sky
promises miracles,

whitewashes the land
where she is waving an angel,

throwing curveballs every which way,
the pure, delicate arcs

bridging the two of them
in a milky circle of light.

IV

Keeping a Net beneath Them

"Teaching is the greatest act of optimism."
—COLLEEN WILCOX

I open the book and pump three poems
into their heads, push a paper ladder
against their brains and beg them
to climb out of their mindset
of common connectivity and fantasy.

But I discover their fear of heights and,
of course, I compete with Facebook,
Twitter, and some strawberry blonde
in a Saran Wrap costume snorkeling for attention.

Once I drowned in the undertow of miniskirts,
bell-bottom trousers, and long hair row after row.
So maybe it makes no difference
what they think or do or wear in school today,
or whether they "squeeze the universe into a ball
to roll it toward some overwhelming question,"
or love "a red wheelbarrow glazed with rainwater
beside the white chickens."

These are the Millennials: the Net Generation
that plumbs the meaning of life without sweetness
and through Wi-Fi networks and iPhones,
and what they learn now surges from a flux
of wireless LAN, Bluetooth, and YouTube.

Perhaps they'll find out later
"all they need to know [about] truth [and] beauty"—
for now, they're just riptides
to their short-circuited obsessions.

Even so, I can't help but love their vertigo
when the heavy tug of ignorance lifts slowly
from their faces against the sinking of gravity,
just after they embark on that first rung
of understanding and ascend
with no sense of balance.

Hell

*"The sinners of the last round
lie completely sealed in ice..."*
—CANTO XXXIV, CIRCLE 9: THE INFERNO

You've heard the jokes
about the insurance salesman and some guy
locked in a soundproof eight-by-ten cell,
or the one about being stalled in traffic
with your mother-in-law and her choir of tongues,
the windows cranked up and with no heat.

In grammar school, the old Irish priest
told us the walls were
"four thousand miles thick,"
that the fire was without seam and everlasting
like a Latin teacher's conjugation of verbs.

But I always thought it was the way
Hieronymus Bosch saw it with special effects,
vapors and strobe lights, or like being trapped
with an eternity of Munch's screamers,
their faces dripping that dripless wax.

Today it's a used-car salesman
who won't give you back your car keys,
or the hail of "Have a nice day" from the cashier
who is buffing her nails and snapping her gum,
you looking up from a circle of ice,
the defroster in your car still not working.

"Have a Nice Day"

I hate it when they say that to me,
always at the doctor's office,
the grocery store, or a restaurant—

this *arrivederci* of the witless,
stoic as a smile button pinned to the lips,
a one-day-only sale I hear all the time

echoing like the syllables of crows.
There's a smell of cheap perfume to it,
like incense at a church service

that keeps me at a distance.
Maybe I should turn the locution
into the kind of dialogue Socrates had

with the soothsayers and Sophists.
Imagine their surprise
as I bring out the truth of their admission

like a gadfly or midwife.
But then again,
maybe Caesar said it best: "You too . . ."

Spilt Milk

I dig the ruins in Rome,
those granite columns, domes,
and arches of megalomania—
the Pantheon, Basilica, and Coliseum.

I am fond of failing love affairs
toppling like dominoes,
one after the other,
where loss becomes gain
and memories tangle
like hair brushed from combs.

I enjoy rained-out baseball games—
swamping a pitcher's mound,
rolling tarpaulins,
the ricochet of lightning
striking the upper deck
like a tape-measured homerun
in a jagged floss of light,
but with Zildjian sound.

I relish cakes that don't rise—
burnt-black dinners, the look
in my wife's smoked-filled eyes,
"Oh, shit!" slipping from her lips.

I cherish old men's faces
worn like dried riverbeds,
their leathery hands,

their hearts profoundly stirred
and the legends they weave
never the same way twice.

But, most of all, I love the second law
of thermodynamics,
the degree of disorder in the world,
and that everything, sooner or later,
will fall apart, cease, and disappear
into energy and collapse into entropy.

Obsession

Lately, I have been eating vast quantities:
York Peppermint Patties, Mounds Bars,
and Reese's Peanut Butter Cups.
While driving, the urge is irresistible.
I make U-turns on one-way streets.
I can't pass Walgreens without stopping
for Ghirardelli Intense Dark
(Twilight Delights with 72% cacao).
I used to be able to pass candy counters,
but now I stop and slobber.
My moans shout, "Behold!"
I can't work without snacking.
My desks are filled with Ritter Sport,
Heath Bars, and Kit Kats.
Every night, I dream about Fannie May
and Godiva.
I wake up humming candy jingles,
then I run sorties at grocery stores.
The checkers want to know what I do
with all that Bosco
at four in the morning.
My wife says she wants a divorce.
The neighbors shake their heads with disbelief.
They keep their children and pets away.
My doctor says I'm depressed
and to just "Fuhgeddaboudit!"
My preacher says to pray to St. Jude;
my dentist says to rinse and floss.

I wish someone would stop me
before I move to Pennsylvania or Côte d'Ivoire—
hand me a cup of hemlock
laced with Ovaltine, or a handful of Toll House chips
mixed with arsenic.

Not Quite a Sonnet on the Divisibility of Kinetics and Infinite Bisection (or a Theory on Yard Work)

I cannot help musing like the ancient
Philosophers, such indolent meta-
Physicians with nothing to do each day:
Hulking Heraclitus with both feet sub-
Merged in the same river, soaking bunions
In a flux to prove his Logos; drunken
Zeno, denying motion by proving
Non-divisibility in goblets
Of wine. All this when there's work to be done:
The grass needs mowing, the hydrangeas need
Trimming. No doubt about this collision
Of leaf and blade. I think I'll leave the lawn
      Half-cut, the boxwoods half-pruned, and ponder
      Other dialectics in my backyard.

Considering a Cat Crossing Highway 435 at 3 a.m. in Kansas City
(or Death Does Not Always Have the Right of Way)

He may have come upon dozens of roadkills himself,
without reflecting upon his nine lives,
or dodged hundreds of Kansas license plates
to return safely to wherever his cat instinct dictated.
But what he was doing on this channel of highway
locked in the crosshairs of my headlight beams
535 miles from Chicago at precisely that moment
my car reeled forward, while juxtaposing cruise control,
refueling and road construction with energy, motion,
and velocity—a colossal calibration
for a near miss—may well have some universal
significance for philosophy or differential calculus.
Call it metaphysics or mathematics.
By any other name, it was luck.

The Checkup
(or A Symphony for a Dental Hygienist)

It's the waiting that intimidates you:
the walls shelved with pamphlets—
root canal treatment, gum disease, X-ray safety.
Then the office door opens like an overture for nerves
when she calls your name.

Your feet, already Novocain numb
from crossing them,
press down the Indian bed of nails
as you walk by the receptionist's counter
to the dental room,
the one with a three-horse-powered vinyl chair
and crane dental light
for a head-and-body tilt devised for excavation.
Of course, there are the instruments,
plastic-wrapped on the metal tray,
alongside the latex gloves and gauzy goggles.

The performance begins with X-rays,
an allegro for two cardboard wings
and your gag reflex;
then your memory is jarred loose
by the scaler, an andante of scraping and foraging
for bacon bits, orange pulp, and toasted crumbs,
your mouth fixed in a capital O
while the saliva ejector hangs from your lower lip,

sucking a maelstrom of spittle,
and the lamp beams down like a car's headlights
just beneath the ceiling tiles and exhaust fan.
There's nowhere else to stare,
except at her face.

By now you know the subtle shades of her eyes
better than you know your wife's—
the blemishes on her brow
and other indelicacies with a Lilliputian scrutiny
as she lavages your mouth with the Cavitron,
con moto moderato, eradicating coffee stains
with a crescendo that rivals timpani.

Finally, you have made it to the finale
of flossing and electric brushing,
an allegretto of rinsing and sucking,
the metallic taste flowing from your molars
and bicuspids raked and plowed clean.

The concert concludes
with the maestro's two-minute coup d'oeil.
"I'll see you in six months" resounds like applause,
and you whisk out the door, vivace!
with toothpaste, brush, and floss in hand,
and with no encore.

Don't Ask Why

"We're going in through here," he says
with a Neil Armstrong drawl,
pointing to a wall chart
of the lower digestive tract.
". . . up the sigmoid and descending colon,
through the transverse, then
down the ascending colon."
Nothing contradictory about that, I think,
"Just four small steps."

Yes, at moments like this,
lunar dust lazes against the slopes of rocks
never before trekked; nebulas remain
unfathomed and quasars unseen.
Here, though, sandblasted by a gallon of CoLyte,
that instant salt and polyethylene punch,
he will see across distant, soft linings
with a myopic pipe of flexible fibers
that beams light to elbow images
back to an eyepiece, milliseconds away.

"We'll take some biopsies," he mutters.
". . . probably just pseudopolyps anyway."
And I'm turned on my left side,
sporting a hospital gown made for such occasions.
Two tubes bullwhip from my nose;
the IV probing my right arm
erases both sensation and memory.

This is something like self-mockery:
life is a hoax, a gift marked by chance
explorations and clichés. Look,
there are black holes sucking light out there
and galaxies exploding at warp speed!
"May the force be with you,"
I murmur before the light goes out.

COVID-19 at the Grocery Store

It is like the Invisible Man
from a long-ago black-and-white film.
But it is not 1933,
and you are not Claude Rains
wearing black velour
against a black velvet background
with double exposure.

You are social distancing
with your face wrapped
in a cloth mask against a background
where bending rays of light
pass from you
into aisles of black beans and chickpeas,
granola bars and breakfast cereals.

And like COVID-19 in its greasy overcoat,
your vest pocket is wet
with Clorox wipes,
and your hands are unexposed
in Nitrile gloves
though you know you are too visible
and afraid of what you cannot see.

Grocery Lists

My wife and I make two lists these days.
We want to cut our time in half at 6 a.m.;
get it done in 40 minutes, or less.

She shops for things more curvy
that spring from the earth:
potatoes, tomatoes, bell peppers . . .
I shop for things sturdier
like cylinders of metal and plastic:
soup cans, coffee, orange juice . . .

It's nothing like the lists
my mother used to make,
the way she would slowly check off
each item social distancing from one another
at the National Food Store
on Chicago and Ashland Avenue:
vegetables and fruits on one side,
dairy and meats on the other.

Nothing quite like today's aisles
of one-way signs
with all of us physical distancing: all of us
looking like outlaws from the Old West,
stagecoach robbers in masks
gripping the sanitized reins
of our shopping carts and galloping out
of the auto checkouts at Jewel
in the nick of time.

"Plaudite, Amici, Comoedia Finita Est"

"Applaud, my friends, for the comedy is finished"
—THE PURPORTED LAST WORDS
OF LUDWIG VAN BEETHOVEN

Shall it be Goethe's "More light! More light!"?
Though Voltaire could hardly distinguish
between a candle and the flames of hell.
I might be more inclined to say something
like Enrico Fermi's "I hope it won't take long,"
or maybe Douglas Fairbanks's quip will do:
"I've never felt better."

But what about, "So little done; so much to do"?
C. J. Rhodes was certainly correct.
And who has done so much in life to believe
Dylan Thomas's "Death shall have no dominion"?

"Dying [of course] is a very dull, dreary affair,"
W. Somerset Maugham said but only once,
and I agree. Indeed,
there will be no fog rising in the distance
or light at the end of some mysterious tunnel.

I can only imagine that great ending lines
come with vision and revision
like Hamlet's "O, I die, Horatio! . . . the rest is silence,"
or Louis XIV's "Why are you weeping?
Did you imagine that I was immortal?"

Or perhaps Socrates's "Crito, I owe a cock
to Asclepius, will you remember to pay the debt?"
Ah, to be so honorable and just at once!

But why should I worry about it after all?
I still have enough time to get it right. Though lately,
Pancho Villa's "[Please] don't let it end like this.
Tell them I said something!"
might do in a pinch.

Without Pomp and Circumstance

Tell them I did not want a church and prayers,
that I believed what a Pulitzer Prize poet once wrote:
"God knows nothing we don't know.
We gave Him every word He ever used."

Tell them I did not want a coffin and flowers either—
that rewind of god-awful dreariness and solemnity,
nor did I want collages or a slideshow. Instead,
share a few of my favorite poems
and play some music, preferably performed,
and have lots of raucous laughter.

Let slip that I once kept a childhood charm,
not owing to superstition or religious belief,
but only because the Vatican had
"Eternally released [Christopher's] duty and sainthood"
when they decided
he was more mythology than reality.
Be sure to tell them how much I loved irony.

Tell them moments are what we are,
that "life is but a day"
and to never "miss out on being alive
in a world where everything is given,
and nothing [is assured]."

But confess to them how I wanted to die
before my wife did, out of fear.
Tell them how I was terrified
of losing a child most of all,
the way some of my dear friends had lost theirs,
and how I worried about the harmful choices
my children sometimes made.

Divulge that dementia was in my family too,
if I had lived long enough
like my grandmother and father,
and how frightened I was about erasing
my identity by cyber crooks,
that it's best to safeguard our money,
as long as "our heart is spent."

Now, tell them how much I loved teaching
and it is through music, poetry,
and philosophy . . . that show us how to be.

Tell them how much I loved to sing
and play Lightfoot and Young . . . on my guitars,
and to listen to Chopin, Mozart, and Bach,
and how I loved the blues and jazz—
when it's bluesy—and reading
Dunn, Collier and Djanikian,
Hume and Camus . . .

Remind them how much I savored
my books, handguns, and Lexuses
(as much as I craved dark chocolate)
and saving unsullied money—
things left behind to prove
this dead collector lived comfortably.

And don't forget to tell them how much
I loved caramel apples and apple fritters . . .
and, of course, my mother,
but not America's hegemony,
bigotry, and hypocrisy.

Proclaim how much I loved my tabbies too,
my dearest friends and family,
and my beautiful selfless wife, Marilyn—
"Forever wilt thou love, and she be fair!"

And that nights filled with stars,
my mother's Calabrian cooking
and sewing machine's hum,
my baseball glove's oily perfume
and the spring's night air,
bright autumn days, the crow's cawing,
the wind's homily swishing through trees,
wind chimes and crunching through leaves
were warm memories of my childhood heart.

At long last, tell them it is old age
who arrives unannounced one day,
emptying its suitcase of inflictions.
And death is the final costume we will all wear
and "nowhere but where it will occur"
and is not mine to keep,
because it will belong to you someday.

So, after all, spin a short yarn,
tell them I said something
unforgettable before I died,
but that you have since forgotten,
though you think I might have whispered
Beethoven's last words:
"Plaudite, amici, comoedia finita est"—
Applaud, my friends, for the comedy is finished —
from my other poem about dying
and my wish to leave an éclat to posterity.

Or was it something else I might have said?
A cliché perhaps?
Like everything of value in life
is revealed through what we loved.

Acknowledgments

Grateful acknowledgments are made to the editors of the following publications in which these poems, sometimes in different versions or titles, first appeared:

American Goat: "Not Quite a Sonnet on the Divisibility of Kinetics and Infinite Bisection," "Peter Stubbs Packs Up and Flees to Chicago via Time Machine to Escape Bad Press," "The Running of the Bulls Festival," "Gifts from God" and "The Day after Vito's Tavern, Father's Day 1957"

Ariel: "Jim's Mom" and "Sanctuary"

California State Poetry Quarterly: "Yes" (from Adverbial Paradoxes)

The Cape Rock: "Birth of an Angel"

Damaged Wine: "Contemplation about a Cat Crossing Highway 435 at 3 a.m.. in Kansas City" and "Snow White Turns 211"

Elf: "Ripped from Space"

Free Inquiry (forthcoming): "Plaudite, Amici, Comoedia Finita Est" and "Without Pomp and Circumstance"

Great River Review: "The Devil's Whore"

Illinois English Bulletin: "Keeping a Net Beneath Them"

The Illinois Review: "Dillinger, Alias Jimmy Lawrence"

Lake Shore Publishing: "Bartleby the Scrivener" and "Suburban Lockup"

Mediphors: "Don't Ask Why"

Negative Capability: "No" (from Adverbial Paradoxes)

New Scriptor: "Paolo and Francesca"

Oyez Review: "Cinderella Dancing"

Pearl: "Riding Rapunzel"

Poet: "Munditia, Patron Saint of Lonely Women"

Poet & Critic: "After an Argument with My Father"

Poetry: "Maybe" (from Adverbial Paradoxes)

Prairie Light Review: "Bubbie," "Have a Nice Day," "Obsession," "It's More than Pheromones," "Hum If You Can't Sing" and "Just Not Fast Enough"

Right Brain Review: "The Billboard" and "Spilt Milk"

South Coast Poetry Journal: "Euclid and Barbie"

Tamaqua: "What Medals Also Mean"

Thorntree Press: "The Iceman Cometh No More," "Because," "Elizabeth Street," "A Small Plot in the Short Story of Our Lives" and "Gray Squirrels, One Robin"

The Spoon River Poetry Review: "Hell," "Briar Rose Defunct," "If Anthony Weiner Had Met Red Riding Hood" and "The Checkup"

Willow Review: "Epitaph for a Transsexual," "Día de los Muertos," "In the Crosshairs" and "Double Vision."

Most of these poems have been revisited and revised from the following collections:

Troika V: "Don't Ask Why" was published by Thorntree Press of which Billy Collins stated: "Glen Brown has a keen ear for the rhythms of American Life and a sharp eye to arrest its images. His poems are driven by the twin engines of wit and genuine feeling, perfectly tuned and balanced."

"Yes, No, Maybe" was published by Lake Shore Publishing of which Neal Bowers stated: "Glen Brown attains what is most difficult in any art, a profound simplicity."

My gratitude to
Marilyn Marie Brown, Robert Borta, Barry Swanson,
Gary Rosenberg, and Carol Killman Rosenberg

About the Author

Glen Brown is a former teacher and long-ago martial artist. He taught creative writing, literature, and philosophy at Lyons Township High School in La Grange, Illinois; composition at the College of DuPage in Glen Ellyn, Illinois; and composition, humanities, poetry, and philosophy at Benedictine University in Lisle, Illinois. He retired after forty-six years of teaching. He now spends his time playing guitar, listening to music, taking walks with his wife, reading poetry, and enjoying his grandchildren.

www.ingramcontent.com/pod-product-compliance
Lightning Source LLC
Chambersburg PA
CBHW032037200426
43209CB00071B/1904/J